PALEO DIET FOR BRITS

The Essential British Paleo Cookbook and Diet Guide

Rockridge Press

Copyright © 2013 by Rockridge Press, Berkeley, California

No part of this publication may be reproduced, stored in a retrieval system or transmitted in any form or by any means, electronic, mechanical, photocopying, recording, scanning or otherwise, except as permitted under Sections 107 or 108 of the 1976 United States Copyright Act, without the prior written permission of the Publisher. Requests to the Publisher for permission should be addressed to the Permissions Department, Rockridge Press, 918 Parker St, Suite A-12, Berkeley, CA 94710.

Limit of Liability/Disclaimer of Warranty: The Publisher and the author make no representations or warranties with respect to the accuracy or completeness of the contents of this work and specifically disclaim all warranties, including without limitation warranties of fitness for a particular purpose. No warranty may be created or extended by sales or promotional materials. The advice and strategies contained herein may not be suitable for every situation. This work is sold with the understanding that the publisher is not engaged in rendering medical, legal or other professional advice or services. If professional assistance is required, the services of a competent professional person should be sought. Neither the Publisher nor the author shall be liable for damages arising herefrom. The fact that an individual, organization or website is referred to in this work as a citation and/or potential source of further information does not mean that the author or the Publisher endorses the information the individual, organization or website may provide or recommendations they/it may make. Further, readers should be aware that Internet websites listed in this work may have changed or disappeared between when this work was written and when it is read.

For general information on our other products and services or to obtain technical support, please contact our Customer Care Department within the U.S. at (866) 744-2665, or outside the U.S. at (510) 253-0500.

Rockridge Press publishes its books in a variety of electronic and print formats. Some content that appears in print may not be available in electronic books, and vice versa.

TRADEMARKS: Rockridge Press and the Rockridge Press logo are trademarks or registered trademarks of Callisto Media Inc. and/or its affiliates, in the United States and other countries, and may not be used without written permission. All other trademarks are the property of their respective owners. Rockridge Press is not associated with any product or vendor mentioned in this book.

ISBN: Print 978-1-62315-161-4 | eBook 978-1-62315-162-1

CONTENTS

Chapter 1: What Is the Paleo Diet? — 1

Chapter 2: Starting Your Paleo Diet — 15

Chapter 3: Set Yourself Up for Success — 29

Chapter 4: Paleo Breakfasts — 34

- Quick Asparagus Egg White Omelette — 34
- Smoked Haddock with Poached Eggs — 36
- Creamed Eggs with Mushrooms — 37
- Smoked Salmon Omelette — 38
- Fluffy Banana Pancakes — 39
- Mixed-Fruit Spread — 40
- Creamy Banana Breakfast Smoothie — 41
- Paleo Green Smoothie — 42
- Paleo Scotch Eggs — 43
- Paleo Coconut and Walnut Pancakes — 44

Chapter 5: Paleo Lunches — 45

- Egg, Bacon and Spinach Salad — 45
- Chicken, Fennel and Orange Salad — 47
- Chicken Liver and Raspberry Salad — 48

Quick Paleo Cock-a-Leekie — 50
Fish and Sweet Potato Chowder — 51
Oven-Roasted Veg and Eggs — 53
Spicy Chicken Masala Curry — 54
Venison and Mushroom Pie — 56
Curried Tuna and Pineapple Salad — 58
Tropical Coronation Chicken — 59

Chapter 6: Paleo Dinners — 60

Deliciously Simple Pot Roast — 60
Easy Barbecued Trout — 62
Garlic- and Lime-Glazed Chicken — 63
Paleo-Friendly Courgette Frittata — 64
Salmon Fillets with Garlic and Dill — 65
Paleo Lancashire Hot Pot — 66
Herb-Grilled Lamb Chops — 67
Pork Chops Glazed with Apple Sauce — 68
Beef and Mushroom Rolls — 69

Chapter 7: Paleo Desserts — 71

Ginger-Glazed Pears with Walnuts — 71
Berrylicious Ice Lollies — 73
Strawberry and Kiwi Granita with Strawberry Sauce — 74
Easy Mango Sorbet — 75
Paleo Pumpkin Pie — 76
Paleo Pear Cakes — 78

    Creamy Vanilla Shake   79
    Berry Tart   80
    Orange Dream Smoothie   81
    Mixed-Fruit Compote   82

Chapter 8: Paleo Snacks   **83**
    Nutty Stuffed Dates   83
    Summer Berry Salad   84
    Curried Fruit and Nut Mix   85
    Sweet Glazed Walnuts   86
    Nutty Banana Lollies   87
    Paleo-Friendly Banana Muffins   88
    Easy Kale Crisps   89
    Banana Chips   90
    Spicy Devilled Eggs   91
    Salmon and Avocado Spread   92
    Paleo Sweet Potato Crisps   93

Paleo Scotch Eggs: Traditional Scotch eggs are made with sausagemeat but Paleo-friendly sausage can be a bit of a hassle to make. This recipe substitutes flavourful pork mince with delicious results.

WHAT IS THE PALEO DIET?

The Paleo diet has become incredibly popular in the past few years, leading many people to assume that it's a new way of eating. In reality, the Paleo diet has been around for almost forty years.

The Origins of the Paleo Diet

In 1975, a gastroenterologist named Dr. Walter Voegtlin published a book called *The Stone Age Diet*. In the book, he documented how he treated patients with a diet that replicated the eating patterns of people during the Paleolithic era. The diet prescribed consuming large quantities of animal fats and proteins and very small quantities of carbohydrates. Dr. Voegtlin reported that his patients, who suffered from disorders such as Crohn's disease and irritable bowel syndrome, showed significant health improvements when following the diet.

Unfortunately, *The Stone Age Diet* did not entirely manage to convince the general public of its benefits. At that time, almost everyone believed that a low-fat, low-calorie diet was the only healthy way to eat.

An Ancient Diet for Modern Times

Despite that initial reception, ten years later Dr. S. Boyd Eaton and Dr. Melvin Konner published a white paper in *The New England Journal of Medicine* that supported Dr. Voegtlin's research. Their paper went on to receive a lot of attention from the medical community and the media. The popularity of this paper about the Paleolithic era diet led to the publication of their book, *The Paleolithic Prescription: A Program of Diet & Exercise and a Design for Living*. This book established the principles that most variations of the Paleo diet follow today.

The book explained the way our Paleolithic ancestors ate and why that nutritional lifestyle was such a healthy one. The most important thing that the authors accomplished was to make the ancient diet suitable for modern times. The book laid out the nutritional content of the original Paleolithic diet and then showed readers how to get that nutritional profile from modern and widely available foods. It was a versatile way in which to eat like our ancestors, and it paved the way for today's Paleo diet phenomenon.

The Paleo Diet for You, the Modern Cave-Dweller

There are several versions of the Paleo diet around today; these versions generally differ in terms of how strictly they follow the eating patterns of our Paleolithic ancestors. The Paleo diet described in this book is a version that is intended to closely duplicate the nutritional composition of a Paleolithic diet without being unrealistic, difficult or complicated. You'll reap the health and weight loss benefits of the Paleo diet without having to turn your entire lifestyle inside out or spend time searching for exotic ingredients. You'll be practising a diet that is moderate in its approach and yet you are likely to experience incredible results.

What the Paleo Diet Looks Like

The Paleo diet is designed to duplicate the results and benefits of our pre-agricultural diet without duplicating the diet's prehistoric methods. While there are a few Paleo followers who do literally hunt, gather or forage all of their food, most people don't have the motivation or time for that level of authenticity. Fortunately, we can achieve the same Paleolithic results with foods readily available to us in grocery stores, health foods stores and farmers markets.

The Paleo diet food pyramid is an inverted version of the one that used to be recommended by the USDA. Meats, eggs and seafood make up the majority of the day's calories, followed by fats from plant foods, fruit and vegetables, and then nuts and seeds. The Paleo diet is a high-protein/low-carbohydrate diet.

In Chapter 2, we'll go into more detail about what you'll be eating from each food group and also give you a specific list of allowed (and disallowed) foods. For the time being, let's establish the basics.

What Is Not on Your Paleo Plate?

The Paleo diet is effective not only because of what you eat, but also because of what you don't eat. Changing the components and proportions of your diet is only half of the Paleo plan. The other half involves eliminating foods that can slow your metabolism down, or which can lead to blood sugar problems, fat storage and sluggish digestion. These eliminated foods include processed food, alcohol, grains, legumes and sugar.

Processed Food

Fast food, frozen or ready meals and store-bought sweets and snacks are not a part of the Paleo diet and should be avoided.

Alcohol

Not only was alcohol an unlikely component of a Paleolithic-era diet, but it is also filled with empty calories and sugar. Alcohol does not supply enough nutritional value to offset its negative dietary attributes, and therefore is not included in the Paleo diet.

Grains

Grains, which include all breads, pasta, rice, oats and barley, are agricultural products whereas you are embarking on a pre-agricultural diet. Later in this chapter, we'll explain in greater detail why grains are strictly off-limits.

Legumes

As with grains, legumes such as beans, peas, soy and soy derivatives are agricultural products and are therefore off-limits. We'll explain the specific risks to your health that these foods pose late in this chapter.

Sugar

One of the remarkable things about the Paleo diet is the impact that it can have not only on lowering blood sugar levels, but also on decreasing your risk of developing diabetes and metabolic syndrome. In part, this is because sugars are eliminated on the Paleo diet. It is also very important to avoid substituting artificial sweeteners for sugar. You can, however, use honey in moderation, as it was likely to have been a part of the ancestral diet.

What Is on Your Paleo Plate?

Meats, Eggs and Seafood

This food group is where you will get most of your calories. All meat, fish, shellfish, mollusks and eggs are allowed, but there are some guidelines for choosing the right foods for the best results. The most important thing is that these foods are of high quality and are prepared with Paleo-approved ingredients.

Fats from Plant Sources

These sources include olives and olive oil, avocadoes (which are a fruit but serve as a fat) and nuts and seeds (which are described in detail in the next section). Since butter is a dairy product and does not improve the health of your heart, it should be avoided when cooking or preparing foods. As a preference, use pure olive oil for cooking and grape-seed oil or extra virgin olive oil for uncooked dressings.

Nuts and Seeds

Nuts and seeds were a big part of the Paleolithic-era diet. All nuts are allowed, with the exception of peanuts, which are a legume. Seeds are allowed, including flax seeds, sunflower seeds, pumpkin seeds, sesame seeds and others. If you are frightened by the idea of giving up pasta and rice, the good news is that quinoa is allowed. Not only is quinoa a seed, but it also makes a great substitute for rice, pasta, oats, barley and other grain foods.

Fruits and Vegetables

The only fruits allowed on the Paleo diet are those that would have been readily available and foraged in the pre-agricultural era. These foraged fruits include berries, such as cranberries, raspberries, strawberries and blueberries. Tree fruits are also a mainstay of the Paleo diet; they include citrus fruits, apples, peaches, plums, cherries, nectarines and pears.

Choose vegetables that can be foraged in the wild. Foraged vegetables include lettuces and leafy greens, tomatoes, peppers, butternut squash, marrow and courgette.

Condiments

Some condiments are allowed, but they should be limited to those that do not contain sugar or any of the forbidden ingredients. Ketchup, for example, is not allowed; mustard, on the other hand, is made from seeds and does not usually contain added sugar. In general, try to rely on herbs and spices rather than condiments.

Beverages

Allowed beverages include pure fruit and vegetable juices, but they should be unsweetened versions and consumed in moderation. Water should be your main drink throughout the day. Tea and coffee are acceptable on the Paleo diet, as long as you use almond milk in them, rather than cow's milk.

Losing Weight on the Paleo Diet

For years, many mainstream dieticians and healthcare providers have touted the benefits of cutting out most meats and oils due to their fat content. They've advised eliminating some fruits and vegetables because of their natural carbohydrate content and strongly advocated eating large quantities of grains and legumes for their high fibre content.

These nutritionists and their diet books have insisted that a diet that is low in calories and fat is the only way to maintain good health and lose weight. However, the research behind the Paleo diet indicates that this is not the case. Paleolithic diet research shows that a diet rich in healthy fats and proteins and low in sugars and starches is not only extremely healthy, but also an excellent way to lose weight. These studies have also indicated that grains and legumes are not the best sources of dietary fibre.

How Does It Work?

You may be wondering: How can I lose weight when I'm still eating meats, fats and high-carb fruits and veggies?

The answer: By using the Paleo methods to align your diet with your body's historical genetic programming, you can boost your metabolic rate, speed your way to healthy and complete digestion, regulate some of the hormones related to energy and fat storage, reduce hunger and curb cravings for unhealthy foods.

The foods you'll be eating on the Paleo diet are the ones which our bodies have been programmed to eat for tens of thousands of years. The foods that you will be eliminating from your diet are foods that we've only been eating for the last one percent of recorded human history; foods that, according to the Paleo diet, are ones that we are not (yet) genetically adapted to eat. These "new" foods slow digestion and metabolism, wreak havoc with our hormones, and cause our bodies to both overeat and store excess fat.

If history serves as a guide, your body needs the good fats, vitamins, minerals, fibre and carbs it gets from meats, fruits and vegetables, nuts and seeds. But it does not need modern grains, legumes or sugars. If you examine the health of the few cultures that still follow this type of diet, you'll see that they are healthier, leaner and tend to live longer than those of us who eat diets heavy in sugar, grains and processed foods.

Why Many Low-Fat, High-Carb Diets Fail

If you're trying to lose weight, the chances are good that this isn't the first time you've tried to do so. Many of us do our best to find the perfect diet and follow it to a T. We may even successfully lose weight for a short time, but do so at the cost of personal comfort—and often at the cost of good health. When you deprive yourself of adequate protein and fats, you're likely to be hungry.

Another problem with mainstream diets is that the grains they recommend are high in starches, which our bodies quickly convert to sugar. The rapid starch-to-sugar conversion process is a common cause of blood sugar spikes, which are quickly followed by blood sugar crashes. These crashes can cause fatigue, lethargy and a craving for more starchy carbohydrates, or carbs, to help pick us back up.

The main problem with these mainstream diets is that many people fail to stick with them for long periods of time. A common reason for this failure is carb-driven cravings. Eliminating carbs, and therefore these cravings, is one of the biggest benefits of the Paleo diet.

Why the Paleo Diet Works

There are a few major differences between how the Paleo diet works and how other diets work. These differences are important because they are likely to directly affect your chances of success in losing weight.

- Low-glycemic carbs that you eat from plant sources can help reduce cravings and increase your energy level.

- High-fibre foods can help keep you full for longer, especially if they don't contain the starches that are found in grains.

- Protein contributes to building lean muscle, which can help you burn fat more quickly.

- Omega-3 fatty acids and other healthy fats can help make you feel full, slow your body's metabolism of sugars, keep your blood sugar levels steady and help you burn stored fat.

- Increased vitamin C from fresh fruits and vegetables, especially berries, can help your body metabolize fat. The process of metabolizing fat results in burning existing stored fat as fuel and using the fat you eat for energy instead of storing it.

- A low-sugar diet can help you avoid insulin resistance and blood sugar level fluctuations. Steadier blood sugar levels can help keep your energy level constant and reduce fatigue.

As these points clearly show, one major benefit of the Paleo diet is that you are unlikely to feel deprived of food or energy. Since the Paleo diet doesn't involve calorie counting, you won't find yourself worrying about a tablespoon of this or a few grams of that. Instead, your primary concern will be to avoid the modern foods that your body can't digest efficiently.

Why You *Need* Fat to *Lose* Fat

Why would you need to eat more fats to lose weight? It's a common question. And the idea that you should eat more dietary fat to lose body fat certainly does sound odd. But it's the *type* of fat you're eating that leads to weight loss (or gain). One type of fat that drives weight loss are the omega-3 fatty acids. These fatty acids are often referred to as "essential" because your body needs them to function properly but is unable to produce them on its own. To get your required amounts of omega-3 fatty acids, you need to either get them from the foods you eat or take a supplement.

One of the main ways omega-3s affect body weight is by regulating insulin production. A common cause of a "belly" or fatty midsection is an insulin-related inability to properly metabolize sugar into glucose, which then fails to be properly converted into glycogen. When the body fails to convert glucose into glycogen, which would then be converted into energy, it stores the excess glucose as fat.

The role of omega-3 fatty acids in this process is to enable the body to produce the chemicals that are necessary to ultimately convert glucose into energy. If you're not getting enough of these essential fatty acids, it becomes more difficult for your body to perform this conversion task optimally. On the Paleo diet, you'll be eating foods laden with omega-3 fatty acids, such as grass-fed meats, seafood, nuts and seeds. While you can get these fatty acids from supplements, incorporating them into your diet naturally is the ideal solution.

Not All Proteins Are the Same

The difference between consuming the processed burgers and sausages that are forbidden on the Paleo diet and the lean steaks and salmon that are recommended could be the difference between being obese or being a leaner, healthier you. There are three main attributes of meat that can affect not only the speed with which you will lose weight, but also your odds of keeping the weight off in the long term.

- **The type and quality of the fats.** Cheap burgers and processed meats such as sausages often have low-quality saturated fats added to them to boost their weight and flavour. While lean steaks and salmon may contain the same amount of fats, they are good fats—the omega-3 fatty acids and other healthy fats your body needs to function properly.

- **The quality and digestibility of the proteins.** Low-grade and processed meats usually contain less protein and are of poor quality. High-quality meat and fish contain high amounts of lean protein that your body can easily extract, digest and use to build muscle.

- **The addition of fillers and preservatives.** Processed meats are typically full of fillers and preservatives that add calories, adversely affect your health and contribute to weight gain. Lean protein such as filet mignon does not contain these additives and preservatives.

By changing the quality of the protein that you eat, you're likely to notice a difference in how you look and feel. You may also lose weight and find that your muscles gain added tone and definition. You'll probably feel fuller longer when you eat high-quality protein, as it takes your body longer to digest it. These are just a few of many incentives for eating the best proteins available.

Summary: Losing Weight on the Paleo Diet

The Paleo diet has several key advantages for people who are looking for a safe, effective way to lose weight and keep it off. The diet recommends consuming lean protein and fat that helps build lean muscle and convert sugar into glycogen that your body can use as energy. It also recommends eliminating sugar, alcohol and processed foods that can make you sick and overweight.

The Paleo diet isn't meant to be a short-term weight loss method. It's a change in lifestyle that many—particularly those previously eating a modern diet—find leads to long-term weight loss.

Better Health with the Paleo Diet

While used by many people today as a way to lose weight, the Paleo diet was originally intended to realign humans with their natural, historical way of eating. As a result of this realignment, the diet's goals were to restore good health and avoid the modern diseases that may be tied to modern diets.

What Is the Theory Behind the Paleo Diet?

The Paleo diet's original creator, Dr. Walter L. Voegtlin, believed that humans aren't genetically designed to digest the modern grains, dairy products, sugars and all of the processed food that we exist on today. Instead, he believed our bodies operate best when running on foods such as lean meat, fish, shellfish, eggs, nuts, veg, fruit and honey—the only foods we consumed and relied on until the Neolithic agricultural revolution approximately 10,000 years ago. Dr. Voegtlin's theory was subsequently supported by the results he saw in his patients and by the decades of respected research that followed.

It's only in the past several thousand years, and in some cases only the past several decades, that we've added sugar, alcohol, grains and engineered and/or processed foods to our diets. As a result, we're suffering from modern diseases commonly referred to as "diseases of affluence" at increasing rates. These diseases are likely the result of our bodies' inability to digest these modern foods.

Preventing or Reversing Metabolic Syndrome

Metabolic syndrome is a group of risk factors that increase the odds of developing diseases such as type 2 diabetes, stroke and heart disease. Risk factors include:

- Extra weight around the waist (for men, a waist of 40 inches or more; for women, 35 inches or more)

- Low HDL cholesterol (for men, under 40 mg/dL; for women, under 50 mg/dL)

- High blood pressure (higher than 130/85 mm Hg)

- High triglycerides (higher than 150 mg/dL)

- High fasting blood sugar (higher than 100 mg/dL)

If three or more of these risk factors are present, you are considered to have metabolic syndrome.

The Paleo diet helps to reduce and/or prevent the incidence of these factors by eliminating the foods shown to contribute to these illnesses, including refined sugar, white flour and processed, fatty food. Combined with increased consumption of lean protein and healthy fats, a decrease in metabolic syndrome risk is likely.

A Healthier Heart

Enabling followers to benefit from a healthier heart is one of the biggest reasons that the Paleo diet has garnered so much attention from the medical community. The lean protein and good fats of the Paleo diet are essential for a healthy heart.

Because the Paleo diet recommends lean meat, shellfish and fish that are low in unhealthy saturated fat, it can help lower bad cholesterol and triglycerides and reduce or potentially reverse arteriosclerosis. Arteriosclerosis is one of the leading causes of stroke, blood clots and aneurysms.

Improved Digestive Health

Because the Paleo diet eliminates most processed grains and legumes, diseases such as colitis, coeliac disease, irritable bowel syndrome and Crohn's disease are less likely to develop, and those with these illnesses may find their symptoms reduced. The diet encourages you to consume fibrous foods such as fruits and vegetables that help flush your digestive system and keep your colon clean and clear. Digestive issues such as diarrhoea, constipation, flatulence, heartburn, acid reflux and gastro-esophageal reflux disease (GERD) are often reduced or eliminated after following the diet for a sustained time period.

Better Immune System

Eliminating foods that our bodies are not genetically equipped to digest will often reduce the incidence of allergies and other immune system issues. You may be surprised to learn that conditions such as lupus, fibromyalgia and rheumatoid arthritis are also considered to be disorders of the immune system. Some patients with these diseases who have switched to the Paleo diet have reported positive results.

The Paleo diet is naturally gluten- and lactose-free; both are substances that some people's bodies treat as allergens. It also eliminates foods that contain other possible allergens, such as antibiotics, preservatives, hormones and dyes. This leaves your immune system increasingly able to fight off disease instead of constantly battling issues caused by foods.

Many people who begin the Paleo diet are not aware that they're suffering from allergic symptoms until they notice that the symptoms have disappeared. Some of these symptoms include frequent headaches, stuffy nose, nausea, swelling of the hands and feet, or general bloating and puffiness. All of these are common immune responses and may go away when you stop exposing your body to the wheat, flour, additives and other ingredients that could be causing them.

2

STARTING YOUR PALEO DIET

In this chapter we'll cover the foods of the Paleo diet in detail, including how and where to shop for them. We'll also show you how to plan Paleo meals day by day, so that you understand what you'll be eating. Finally, we'll discuss some tips to help make your transition to the Paleo diet a smooth, enjoyable and successful one.

What You'll Be Eating on the Paleo Diet

Much of the success of the Paleo diet lies not only in the types of foods you eat, but also the quality of those foods. Our ancestors ate wild foods that were of high quality and free of chemicals, hormones and many other ingredients that have made the modern diet largely unhealthy.

For most people, the idea of raising, hunting and/or foraging for their own food is unrealistic. Many people also lack the budget for unusual (and often therefore expensive) ingredients. Taking these considerations into account, the following guidelines recommend Paleo-approved foods that are realistic to find and purchase. Later in the chapter, we'll explain how to find these foods in your local supermarket and through other local resources.

Animal and Fish Proteins

Animal and fish proteins make up the majority of the Paleo diet. I recommend purchasing the highest quality proteins that you can reasonably afford. If game, exotic meat like buffalo, and wild salmon are too expensive for your budget, rest assured that grass-fed beef, organic chicken and fresh or frozen prawns are just as good.

The Paleo diet recommends that livestock meats such as beef, buffalo, ostrich, pork and lamb are grass-fed, organic and free of any hormones or antibiotics. You are also encouraged to eat wild meat and game, such as deer and boar. When considering which cuts of meat to buy, lean cuts are preferred to cuts with a high fat content.

Poultry should be organic, vegetarian-raised and free of hormones. Chicken, turkey, duck, goose and Cornish hens are good Paleo options. Eggs are also an easy and excellent source of protein on the Paleo diet, but they should be from free-range, organic birds.

Your seafood choices are numerous. You can eat all kinds of fish, prawns, crab, clams, oysters, lobster and other crustaceans and molluscs. I recommend prioritising cold-water fish varieties such as cod, haddock, mackerel and salmon to maximize your omega-3 consumption.

You can prepare your meat, poultry and seafood by steaming, broiling, grilling, sautéing, pan-frying, baking or broiling. As you may suspect, it is best to avoid deep frying, because neither batter nor the typical deep frying oils are recommended.

Fruit and Vegetables

There are a large number of delicious fruits and vegetables to choose from. In general, you can eat any fruits and vegetables other than corn and most root vegetables, which have a high sugar and starch content. Your Paleo diet excludes potatoes, beets, turnips and parsnips. Carrots can be eaten in moderation and onions are historically a wild crop and therefore acceptable.

Try to select low-glycemic fruits and vegetables for most of your meals and snacks. In doing so, you'll be more likely to maintain an even blood sugar level and have a steadier source of energy.

Whenever possible, the fruit and vegetables that you purchase (including mushrooms and other plant foods) should be organic and in season. This ensures that they are as healthy, nutritious and delicious as possible. Frozen fruits and vegetables are allowed, but you should keep them to a minimum. Canned fruits and vegetables are typically overcooked and over-salted, and should be avoided.

Nuts, Seeds and Oils

Nuts, seeds and oils are an important part of the Paleo diet. They supply healthy fats, fibre and a feeling of fullness that can help keep you from being besieged by unhealthy cravings.

Allowed nuts include tree nuts, such as pecans, walnuts and almonds. Peanuts are a legume and are therefore not allowed. Nuts should be eaten raw as often as possible; if you prefer roasted nuts, make sure they're roasted without sugar, salt or added oil. Seeds such as pumpkin seeds, sunflower seeds, squash seeds and sesame seeds make great snacks, and flax seed or flax seed oil is loaded with healthy fats and antioxidants.

Use extra virgin olive oil for making dressings, as a substitute for butter on veggies and for cooking foods at low heat. Use pure olive oil or grape-seed oil for cooking at medium to high temperatures.

8 Tips for Success: Planning Your Paleo Diet

Knowing what to eat is half the key to success; knowing how and when to eat it is the other half. The guidelines for the Paleo diet are intended to be simple, because complicated diets rarely succeed.

1. Don't Count Calories

Calorie counting or portioning are not a part of the Paleo diet. The Paleo diet is a natural way of eating what your body was designed to eat; Paleolithic people often consumed a much higher number of calories and fat grams than most diets allow. Once you see the results, calorie counting will no longer be a part of your vocabulary.

On the Paleo diet, you should feel less hunger due to an increased consumption of healthy fats, lean protein and fibre. If you eat only when you're hungry, you're likely to avoid overeating without having to count calories.

2. The Proper Ratio of Protein to Carbs

You should try to maintain a proper ratio between your protein intake and your carb intake. The easiest way to keep this ratio in line is by looking at your menu and your plate. For all meals, at least half your plate should be protein, and half or less should be fruit, veg, nuts and seeds.

In general, your daily diet should consist of fifty-five to sixty-five percent protein, thirty to forty percent carbs, and five percent non-animal fats such as those found in nuts, seeds, avocadoes and olive oil. If you feel your energy level is dragging when you first start the diet, try increasing your carb consumption. If you find yourself snacking all day and still feeling hungry, try increasing your protein consumption.

It may take a few weeks for your body to adjust to the way it converts food into energy. For the first week or two, you are likely to find yourself craving the carbs and quick energy of pasta, bread or a bowl of cereal. It's normal for your energy level to dip the first couple of weeks, but it should increase as your body begins to increasingly use protein as a source of energy.

3. Planning Your Daily Diet

I recommend that you eat at least three main meals a day and several healthy snacks in between. Try to avoid going more than two hours without at least some lean protein. Snacking will keep hunger away and keep your blood sugar levels steady.

Even if you're not inclined to plan your menus in advance, many people find that doing so increases their initial chances of success. It's important to have what you need on hand so that you don't fall for unhealthy temptations.

After a couple of weeks on the diet, you'll have a better understanding of how and when to eat and likely find it easier to create your own meal plans. To get started, here are some guidelines to help you achieve the best results.

4. Early Morning/Breakfast

Eat as soon as possible after you wake up, especially during your first few weeks on the Paleo diet. If you keep your evening meals protein-heavy and light on carbs, you may awaken with more energy in the morning.

Scrambled eggs and omelets are good breakfast choices if you have time to cook. If you don't have time in the morning, cold leftover meats and protein smoothies are good Paleo options.

5. Lunch

Lunch should include a large serving of protein, such as a meat stew, cold leftover chicken, or a salad with chicken breast or prawns. Add some high-fibre carbs such as a salad or fruit with a handful of nuts to feel more full and energetic.

6. Dinner

Your evening meals should focus primarily on protein. Most people burn less energy during the evening. Unless you work out after dinner, try to limit your carb intake. Choose low-glycemic veggies as your side dishes.

7. Dessert or Evening Snack

You're free to choose between a sweet treat or a little more of what you had for dinner. Fruit, unsweetened sorbets or any of the Paleo-friendly dessert recipes included later in this book can satisfy your sweet tooth.

8. Snacks

Throughout your day, you should snack as frequently as possible—at least once every two to three hours. Focus on a mix of both protein and carbs for each snack. The protein will help keep you from getting hungry and the carbs will help you avoid fatigue. Eating frequently can also speed up your metabolism.

Paleo-Recommended Foods

Meat

- Eggs (from chicken, duck or geese; do not buy egg substitutes)
- Game
  - Duck
  - Buffalo
  - Goose
  - Grouse
  - Ostrich
  - Partridge
  - Pheasant
  - Quail
  - Rabbit
  - Reindeer
  - Squab
  - Turtle
  - Venison

- - Wild boar
  - Wild turkey
- Goat (any cut)
- Lean beef (trimmed of visible fat)
  - Braising steak
  - Sirloin steak
  - Extra lean mince (seven percent fat or less)
  - Rump steak
  - Lean veal
  - Frying steak
- Lean pork (trimmed of visible fat)
  - Pork loin
  - Pork chops
- Lean poultry (white meat, skin removed)
  - Chicken breast
  - Turkey breast
  - Partridge breast
- Organ meats
  - Beef, lamb, pork and chicken livers and kidneys
  - Chicken and turkey gizzards and hearts
  - Beef, pork and lamb tongues
  - Beef, pork and lamb marrow
  - Beef, pork, lamb and veal sweetbreads
- Rabbit (any cut)

Fish

- Seabass
- Bluefish
- Cod
- Eel
- Grouper
- Haddock

- Halibut
- Herring
- Mackerel
- Monkfish
- Mullet
- Northern pike
- Orange roughy
- Perch
- Red snapper
- Rockfish
- Salmon
- Sardine (packed in olive oil or water)
- Scrod
- Shark
- Striped bass
- Sunfish
- Swordfish
- Tilapia
- Trout
- Tuna
- Turbot
- Walleye
- Any other commercially available fish

Seafood

- Abalone
- Brown shrimp
- Clam
- Cockles
- Crab
- Crayfish
- Lobster

- Mussels
- Oysters
- Prawns
- Scallops

Fruit

- Apple
- Apricot
- Avocado
- Banana
- Blackberry
- Boysenberry
- Blueberry
- Cantaloupe melon
- Cherry
- Cranberry
- Gooseberry
- Grape
- Grapefruit
- Guava
- Honeydew melon
- Kiwi
- Lemon
- Lime
- Lychee
- Mango
- Nectarine
- Orange
- Papaya
- Passion fruit
- Peach

- Pear
- Persimmon
- Pineapple
- Plum
- Pomegranate
- Raspberry
- Rhubarb
- Star fruit
- Tangerine
- Watermelon

Vegetables

- Artichoke
- Asparagus
- Aubergine
- Beet greens
- Bell pepper
- Broccoli
- Brussels sprouts
- Cabbage
- Cauliflower
- Celeriac
- Celery
- Chilli
- Chinese greens (pak choi, bok choi etc)
- Courgette
- Cucumber
- Dandelion greens
- Endive
- Kale
- Kohlrabi
- Lettuce (except iceberg)

- Mushroom
- Mustard greens
- Onion
- Parsley
- Pumpkin
- Seaweed
- Spinach
- Spring onion
- Squash (all kinds)
- Swiss chard
- Tomato
- Turnip
- Watercress

Nuts, Seeds and Oils

- Almond butter
- Almond
- Brazil nut
- Cashew
- Chestnut
- Coconut oil
- Flax seed
- Hazelnut
- Macadamia nut
- Nut flour (almond and hazelnut are recommended)
- Olive oil
- Pecan
- Pine nut
- Pistachio
- Pumpkin seeds
- Sesame seeds

- Sunflower seeds
- Sesame butter or tahini (pure and raw)
- Walnut

Beverages

- Fruit juice (pure and organic, without any added sugar)
- Green tea
- Herbal tea
- Water

Other

- Carob powder
- Coconut flour and milk
- Dried fruit without added sugar
- Fresh and dried herbs
- Frozen fruit and fruit bars without added sugar
- Raw, organic honey
- Spices and seasonings

Foods to Avoid on the Paleo Diet

Dairy

- All food made with any dairy products
- Butter
- Cheese
- Dairy spreads
- Frozen yoghurt
- Ice cream

- Low-fat milk
- Non-fat dairy creamer
- Powdered milk
- Skimmed milk
- Whole milk
- Yoghurt

Cereal Grains

- Barley (barley soup, barley bread and all processed foods made with barley)
- Buckwheat
- Corn (corn on the cob, corn tortillas, corn chips, cornstarch and corn syrup)
- Millet
- Oats (includes rolled oats and all processed foods made with oats)
- Rice (brown rice, white rice, rice noodles, basmati rice, rice cakes, rice flour and all processed foods made with rice)
- Rye (rye bread, rye crackers and all processed foods made with rye)
- Wheat (bread, biscuits, rolls, muffins, noodles, crackers, doughnuts, pancakes, waffles, pasta, wheat tortillas, pizza, pitta bread, flat bread and all processed foods made with wheat or wheat flour)

Legumes

- All beans (black beans, broad beans, fava beans, green beans, kidney beans, lima beans, mung beans, pinto beans, red beans, string beans and white beans)
- Black-eyed peas
- Chickpeas
- Lentils
- Mangetout

- Miso
- Peanuts and peanut butter
- Peas
- Snow peas
- Soybeans and all soy products, including tofu

Starchy Vegetables

- Cassava root
- Potatoes and all potato products (such as French fries and potato chips)
- Tapioca
- Yams

High-Salt Meats and Snacks

- Bacon (use the lean portions occasionally for seasoning when cooking)
- Chorizo
- Deli meats
- Hot dogs
- Ketchup
- Nearly all canned meats and/or fish
- Pickled foods
- Pork scratchings
- Processed meats
- Salami
- Salted nuts
- Salted spices
- Sausages, fresh or smoked
- Smoked, dried and salted fish and meat

3

SET YOURSELF UP FOR SUCCESS

Any diet requires the right mindset and attitude to succeed. In this chapter, we'll give you the tools to get motivated, enthusiastic and ready to begin the Paleo diet.

Getting into the Right Mindset

Making a significant change in your habits and lifestyle is never easy. To succeed, two of the most important things you'll need are the right attitude and the right reasons for making the change.

Doing things for others is admirable, but changing your diet should be for you. If you're trying to lose weight because you want someone else's approval, you may be setting yourself up for failure. After all, the opinions of others simply may not be enough to keep you on track when times get hard. Ideally, your focus should be on how you want to look and feel and on improving your quality of life. Admiration from others should be merely a bonus.

The first couple of weeks of the Paleo diet are likely to require determination, willpower and commitment. For some people, the Paleo diet will require a significant change in their eating patterns. For others, their energy levels may be lower in the first few weeks. To increase your chances of success, prepare yourself for these realities.

Beginning the Paleo diet is the hardest part. Once you see and feel the results, you're likely to have all the motivation you need.

What Kind of Caveman Are You?

This quick quiz will help you understand how your lifestyle, habits and personality might affect your experience on the Paleo diet. Once you've worked out your answers, we'll provide some practical tips to help you succeed.

1. *Which best describes you?*
    a) I don't particularly like to cook, and I eat ready meals or eat out often.
    b) I'm a fairly good cook, but I don't have much time to do so during the week.
    c) Cooking is okay, but I'm not very good at it.
    d) I live to cook and I consider it one of my favourite pastimes.

2. *Are you more likely to:*
    a) Spend a lot of your free time away from home.
    b) Spend most evenings at home, tired and stressed from a busy day.
    c) Spend most evenings at home working or taking care of the kids.
    d) Entertain friends and family on weekends and during the week.

3. *Do you like to:*
    a) Try new things as long as you don't have to cook them.
    b) Keep your menu quick and simple.
    c) Stick with cooking simple basics that you know how to prepare.
    d) Try new recipes and cuisines at home.

4. In the mornings do you:
   a)   Usually stop for breakfast on the way to work.
   b)   Tend to skip breakfast and overeat later.
   c)   Grab a breakfast bar or muffin at work.
   d)   Always have breakfast.

If you answered A for most of the questions:

Find a few restaurants to eat at regularly that serve lean steaks, fresh seafood (not fried) and fresh vegetables and salads. Ask your waiter not to offer the bread basket, drink plenty of water and keep your protein-carb ratio in mind.

Be careful of skipping meals while you're away from home, especially at work. Bring cold roast chicken, salads, fresh fruit and nuts to work for handy and healthy snacks.

If you answered B for most of the questions:

Your main priority when starting the Paleo diet is going to be managing your time. Your main obstacle will be resisting the urge to grab the wrong foods because you're tired or hurried. Spend some time on the weekend preparing large batches of food for the week. This can be as simple as baking chicken legs, boiling prawns or bagging up your own mix of nuts and dried fruit. If you have healthy meals ready to eat when you're hungry during the week, you'll be less likely to grab whatever is handy.

If you answered C for most of the questions:

Combining healthy prepared foods with some simple homemade dishes may be your best bet. An example of a healthy prepared food might be rotisserie chicken with the skin removed. A simple homemade dish could be a basic soup recipe that you make in large quantities and freeze for later, or a protein smoothie for breakfast.

If you answered D for most of the questions:

You have an advantage because you'll be able to keep meals exciting by trying lots of new ingredients and recipes. You may want to prepare a number of dishes once a week and store or freeze them to eat at work or on busier evenings. If you're cooking for your non-Paleo family in the evenings, don't try to make two meals; instead, just skip the starch or grain they're eating and pile extra proteins and veggies onto your plate.

Making the Transition

There are a number of things you can do to help ease your transition to the Paleo diet and make it enjoyable. Much like the process of preparing for a holiday, you'll want to have a plan for what you'll be doing and make sure you have everything you need. Here are some tips for making your transition as smooth and simple as possible.

Find New Food Sources

Do some research to decide where and how you'll be doing your food shopping. There are great sources available both locally and online; try to identify these sources before you get started. If you're going to be using online food resources, you'll need to order ahead of time to make sure you have those foods on hand for your first week.

Spread the Word

It's a good idea to prepare the people around you for your lifestyle change. This will enable them to support you and help to avoid unintended temptation from friends who may not know that you're making a change.

In particular, it's very important to prepare housemates and family members for the changes you're making. They don't have to join you or even agree with you, but they should be supportive and respectful. Talk to them before you get started and let them see that you're excited. They'll be much more likely (and able) to encourage and help you.

The First Few Weeks

Take care to avoid your dietary weak spots. Skip drinking at happy hour with your office buddies and join them for a healthy lunch instead. Go for a walk instead of sitting in front of the TV after dinner.

You might want to keep an informal journal of how you feel and what you eat during your first couple of weeks. It can be motivating and educational. As you see and feel the changes in your body, take note. These observations can help keep you on track later if you hit a rough spot.

4

PALEO BREAKFASTS

Quick Asparagus Egg White Omelette

Serves two.

If you prefer to use just egg whites, this omelette recipe will soon become one of your favourite dishes. It's great for breakfast, but it is equally delicious for lunch or dinner.

- 200g asparagus, trimmed
- ½ teaspoon salt
- ½ teaspoon freshly ground black pepper
- 8 egg whites, beaten
- ½ teaspoon olive oil

Using a steamer or a sieve positioned over a medium saucepan, bring 4 cups of water to a boil and steam the asparagus for 7–8 minutes until it is tender but still retains a little bite.

Drain the asparagus and then season with salt and pepper while warm.

Whisk the egg whites in a medium mixing bowl until frothy.

Heat the oil over medium-high heat in a nonstick frying pan. Pour in the eggs, reduce the heat to medium-low and cook for 2–3 minutes, until the bottom is set.

Carefully flip the omelette and place the asparagus on the nearest half. Fold the far half over to create a half-moon shape and slide the omelette onto a plate.

To serve, cut in half and serve hot.

Smoked Haddock with Poached Eggs

Serves four.

Smoked haddock lends just the right smoky flavour to offset the creaminess of the eggs. Together, they're a perfect breakfast combination.

- 2 small fillets undyed smoked haddock, about 175g each
- 275ml coconut milk
- 4 large eggs
- 2 teaspoons vinegar
- ½ teaspoon freshly ground black pepper

Rinse the haddock, pat it dry with kitchen paper and cut each fillet in half to make 4 pieces. Place skin side down in a large pan and add just enough milk to cover. Place pan over medium-high heat.

Bring to a boil, cover, reduce the heat to low and simmer for 5–6 minutes until the fish flakes easily with a fork.

Meanwhile, fill a large saucepan 1/3 full of water and place on medium-high heat. Add the vinegar and bring water to a simmer. Reduce heat to medium-low.

Break the eggs into a small bowl one at a time, then use a whisk to vigorously swirl the simmering water into a whirlpool as you pour each egg into the centre of the pan. Simmer for 4 minutes, or until lightly set.

Drain the cooked fish fillets on kitchen paper, and then transfer to serving plates, skin side down. Place a poached egg on each fillet, sprinkle with black pepper and serve.

Creamed Eggs with Mushrooms

Serves two.

This Paleo-friendly version of a classic breakfast and brunch dish is every bit as delicious as the traditional version. The mushrooms will keep well in the fridge for up to four days, so feel free to prepare them ahead of time.

- 2 teaspoons coconut oil, divided
- 1 onion, finely chopped
- 1 clove garlic, crushed
- 225g chestnut mushrooms, finely chopped
- Pinch of freshly grated nutmeg
- 1 teaspoon chopped thyme
- 1 tablespoon chopped parsley
- ½ teaspoon salt, divided
- ¼ teaspoon freshly ground black pepper
- 4 large eggs, beaten

Melt 1 teaspoon of the coconut oil over medium heat in a heavy saucepan. Add the onion and garlic and sweat them, stirring frequently for about 3–4 minutes or until translucent.

Add the mushrooms, cover and cook for an additional 5 minutes, stirring occasionally.

Add the nutmeg, thyme, parsley, ¼ teaspoon salt and the pepper. Remove to a bowl and cover to keep warm. Wipe out the pan.

Melt the remaining coconut oil over low heat and add the eggs. Season with the remaining salt. Cook for 3–4 minutes or just until they start to set. Add the mushroom mixture and remove from heat.

Continue stirring the eggs and mushrooms until creamy. Serve immediately over a slice of Paleo-friendly toast.

Smoked Salmon Omelette

Serves two.

Smoked salmon can be quite expensive, but a little bit goes a long way in this delicious omelette. Make this for weekend guests or as a quick supper.

- 1 teaspoon olive oil
- 4 large eggs
- ¼ teaspoon salt
- ¼ teaspoon freshly ground black pepper
- 55g smoked salmon
- 2 tablespoons chopped chives

Heat a 25cm omelette pan over medium-high heat. Add the olive oil.

Break the eggs into a small bowl and beat lightly with a fork or whisk.

When the oil is hot, add the salt and pepper to the eggs and pour half of the mixture into the pan. Gently poke holes into the egg with a fork until it begins to set.

Flip the eggs carefully with a spatula and add half of the salmon and chives. Using a spatula, fold one side into the centre, then tilt the pan and fold over the other side. Slide onto a plate and cover to keep warm. Repeat with the remaining ingredients to make the second omelette.

Fluffy Banana Pancakes

Makes four pancakes.

Pancakes are a breakfast favourite, especially for families with children. This recipe makes a small batch just perfect for a cool morning. These will keep well in the fridge, so make a double batch and reheat them as needed for busy mornings.

- 2 bananas
- 200ml coconut milk
- 4 tablespoons ground almonds
- 1 tablespoon raw honey
- 3 eggs
- ½ teaspoon vanilla extract
- ½ teaspoon nutmeg
- 2 tablespoons coconut oil

Mix all ingredients except the coconut oil in a blender. Blend on medium speed until well blended.

Melt half of the oil in a medium frying pan over medium heat. Pour a quarter of the batter into the pan and cook until slightly dry in the centre and then turn to cook the other side.

Repeat with the rest of the batter, adding extra coconut oil if needed. Serve hot with maple syrup or warm raw honey.

Mixed-Fruit Spread

Serves about twenty.

This delicious spread made with several fruits is a great alternative to butter, peanut butter or sugary jams. Enjoy it as a topping for Paleo-friendly pancakes or muffins or in a sandwich with some almond butter.

- 500g cooking apples (such as Bramleys) peeled, cored and diced
- 250g dried apricots
- 250g dried figs
- 500ml apple juice
- ½ teaspoon cinnamon
- ¼ teaspoon nutmeg
- 1½ teaspoons lemon juice, or to taste

Place the apples, apricots, figs, apple juice, cinnamon and nutmeg into a heavy saucepan. Set the pan over a high heat and bring to a boil, stirring occasionally.

Reduce the heat to low and simmer, uncovered, for 30 more minutes or until the mixture has become pulp and no liquid remains on the surface. Stir frequently to prevent the fruit from sticking to the bottom of the saucepan.

Remove from the heat and allow the mixture to cool for 10–15 minutes before adding lemon juice to taste.

Pour the cooled fruit mixture into a food processor or blender and process on medium speed until it resembles a thick purée.

Cool completely before serving. The spread can be kept in an airtight container in the refrigerator for up to 2 weeks.

Creamy Banana Breakfast Smoothie

Serves two.

Even if you barely have a moment to spare in the mornings, you can still have a delicious and healthy breakfast. You can whip up this smoothie in a hurry and you can drink it on the go if you need to.

- 2 bananas
- 225ml almond milk
- 4 tablespoons water
- 2 tablespoons raw honey
- 8 ice cubes

Place all of the ingredients, except for the ice cubes, into a blender. Blend on high until smooth. Add the ice cubes and blend again until thick and creamy.

Paleo Green Smoothie

Serves two.

Green smoothies provide you with a ton of vitamins and minerals from green veggies and fruits. This recipe will be a delicious start to your day and takes just a couple of minutes to prepare.

- 1 cup fresh spinach
- 1 cup fresh watercress
- 500ml unsweetened apricot nectar
- 1 banana

Place all ingredients in a blender and blend on high for 1–2 minutes until very smooth. Drink immediately.

Paleo Scotch Eggs

Serves four.

Traditional Scotch eggs are made with sausagemeat and Paleo-friendly sausage can be a bit of a hassle to make. This recipe substitutes pork mince with delicious results.

- 4 large eggs
- 500g fresh pork mince
- ½ teaspoon salt
- ½ teaspoon freshly ground black pepper
- ½ cup chopped fresh parsley
- ½ teaspoon dried rosemary
- 1 tablespoon coconut oil

Place the eggs in a saucepan of cold water to cover and bring to a boil over a high heat. Cover, remove from the heat and allow them to steep for 15 minutes. Place in a bowl of cold water to cool.

In a large mixing bowl, combine the pork mince, salt, pepper, parsley and rosemary and mix well with clean hands.

Divide the mince into 4 patties about 2cm thick.

Peel the eggs and place 1 egg in the centre of each patty. Use your hands to mold the patty around the egg, taking care that there are no gaps or tears.

Preheat the oven to 180 C / Gas Mark 4 and heat the coconut oil in a large frying pan.

Brown the eggs on all sides for about 10 minutes total, then place into a baking dish and bake for another 15 minutes.

Paleo Coconut and Walnut Pancakes

Makes four to six pancakes.

These pancakes are loaded with nuts and their healthy fats, which will provide you with plenty of energy to get through your busiest mornings. These will keep in the fridge for up to four days, so make extra to pop into the microwave on hectic days.

- 2 tablespoons coconut flour
- 500ml coconut milk
- 4 large eggs
- 250ml water
- 1 teaspoon cinnamon
- 1 cup of chopped walnuts
- 3 teaspoons coconut oil

Place the coconut flour, coconut milk, eggs, water and cinnamon in a blender and blend on a low speed until smooth. Pour into a measuring jug.

Stir in the walnuts.

Heat 1 teaspoon of the coconut oil in a large heavy frying pan over medium-high heat. Pour in enough batter to make a 10cm pancake. Cook until the centre is almost dry, about 3 minutes, then turn. Cook for 1 more minute, then place on a covered plate to keep warm.

Repeat with the remaining batter. Serve hot with maple syrup or raw honey.

5

PALEO LUNCHES

Egg, Bacon and Spinach Salad

Serves two as a main course.

This quick salad recipe is loaded with flavour yet has just a few ingredients. You can prepare it in a hurry or, if you like, prepare it the night before and store it undressed in the fridge for several days.

- 4 large eggs
- 8 rashers uncured, unsmoked bacon or pancetta
- 300g fresh spinach
- 1 small onion, chopped
- 6 tablespoons olive oil
- 3 tablespoons lemon juice
- 2 cloves garlic, crushed
- ¼ teaspoon salt
- ¼ teaspoon freshly ground black pepper

Place the eggs in a saucepan with enough cold water to cover. Bring the water to the boil; cover, remove from heat and let eggs stand for 10–12 minutes. Drain and place in a bowl of cold water to cool. Once cool, peel and chop the eggs and set aside.

Meanwhile, heat a large heavy frying pan over a medium-high heat and cook the bacon until evenly browned, turning once. Drain on some kitchen towels, then chop and set aside.

In a medium bowl, mix together the eggs, bacon, spinach and onion.

In a separate small bowl, whisk together the oil, lemon juice, garlic, salt and pepper. Pour over the salad and toss well to coat.

Chicken, Fennel and Orange Salad

Serves two as a main course or four as a starter.

This recipe is a take on a traditional Italian salad, with added protein from the chicken breast. To save time, prepare a few extra breasts for dinner the night before and then dice them before storing in the fridge.

- 500g cooked chicken breast, diced
- 1 bulb fennel, trimmed and sliced
- 2 large oranges, peeled and sliced into rounds
- 100g wild rocket, chopped
- 2 tablespoons olive oil
- 2 tablespoons red wine vinegar
- 1 teaspoon poppy seeds
- Salt and pepper, to taste

In a medium bowl, combine the chicken, fennel and oranges.

In a small measuring jug, whisk together the olive oil, red wine vinegar, poppy seeds, salt and pepper and pour over the salad. Toss well to coat and refrigerate for 1 hour or more.

Remove the fennel mixture from the fridge and add the rocket. Toss again to coat and serve cold.

Chicken Liver and Raspberry Salad

Serves four as a main course.

The flavour combination may sound odd, but this is a classic French bistro recipe that has to be tasted to be appreciated. When raspberries are out of season, try this with fresh strawberries, which is equally delicious.

- 400g chicken livers
- 150g mixed lettuce leaves, such as Oak Leaf and Romaine
- 100g baby spinach leaves
- 4 tablespoons chopped fresh parsley
- 4 tablespoons snipped fresh chives
- 3 tablespoons olive oil, divided
- 100g shallots, finely chopped
- 1 large clove garlic, crushed
- 3 tablespoons raspberry vinegar
- 125g raspberries
- Salt and pepper, to taste

Trim the chicken livers, removing any membrane tissue. Cut large pieces in half. Pat the chicken livers dry with some kitchen paper, then set aside.

Mix together the lettuce, spinach, parsley and chives and set aside as well.

Heat 2 tablespoons of the olive oil in a large frying pan over a medium heat. Add the shallots and garlic and cook for about 2 minutes or until softened, stirring frequently.

Increase the heat to medium-high and add the remaining tablespoon of olive oil to the pan. Add the chicken livers and cook, stirring frequently, for about 5 minutes or until they are ready. Test 1 piece by cutting it in half. There should be just a hint of pink in the centre.

Add the raspberry vinegar to the pan and stir, scraping up any browned bits from the bottom. Season the mixture with the salt and pepper to taste.

Remove from the heat and allow it to cool until very warm, but no longer hot. Pour the liver mixture over the salad, top with the berries and serve immediately.

Quick Paleo Cock-a-Leekie

Serves four.

You won't miss the rice in this version of the classic British soup. The addition of chopped frozen cauliflower lends it just the right texture and heartiness, without changing the flavour.

- 1 tablespoon olive oil
- 270g boneless, skinless chicken thighs, chopped
- 2 leeks (about 350g), trimmed and washed
- 1.2 litres chicken stock
- 1 bouquet Garni (fresh or dried)
- 8 prunes, chopped
- ½ teaspoon salt
- ¼ teaspoon freshly ground black pepper
- 1 box (about 350g) frozen cauliflower, thawed and chopped finely
- 2 tablespoons chopped fresh parsley to garnish

In a large non-stick saucepan, heat the oil over a medium-high heat. Add the chicken to the pan and sauté for 5 minutes, stirring often until evenly browned all over. Remove from the pan and drain on kitchen paper.

Trim away the green parts of the leeks and set aside. Cut the white parts into slices and add the sliced leeks to the pan. Fry for 5 minutes or until soft, stirring frequently.

Add the stock and bouquet Garni to the pan and add the chicken once more. Season with salt and pepper, then bring to the boil. Reduce the heat to low, cover and simmer for 30 minutes or until the chicken is tender.

Slice the green parts of the leeks finely, then add them to the pan, along with the prunes and chopped cauliflower. Cover and simmer for an additional 10 minutes.

Remove the bouquet Garni, ladle the soup into shallow bowls and garnish with some chopped fresh parsley.

Fish and Sweet Potato Chowder

Serves four.

The combination of briny fish and delicate sweet potato makes this chowder a winner. Cook this on a weekend to keep for some tasty work lunches!

- 100g smoked haddock
- 100g unsmoked haddock
- 500ml coconut milk
- 500ml seafood stock
- 2 sprigs fresh thyme
- ¼ teaspoon freshly ground black pepper
- ¼ teaspoon nutmeg
- 1 teaspoon coconut oil
- 1 onion, finely chopped
- 1 leek, sliced
- 1 clove garlic, finely chopped
- 1 stalk celery, sliced thinly
- 1 large carrot, sliced thinly
- 1 large sweet potato, peeled and diced

Place a large, heavy saucepan over a medium-high heat and place both types of fish, skin on, into the bottom. Add the coconut milk, seafood stock, thyme, nutmeg, and pepper. Bring to a boil, then remove from the heat and allow to sit for 1 hour.

After an hour, remove the fish from the liquid, remove the skin and any small bones and tear into bite-sized (no smaller) pieces. Set aside to be added at the end. Remove the thyme sprigs from the cooking liquid and discard them.

Heat the coconut oil in a large pan over a medium-high heat. Add the onions, leek, garlic, celery and carrots and sauté just until soft, about 10 minutes.

Pour vegetables into the cooking liquid, and add the sweet potato.

Bring to a boil and then reduce the heat to low and simmer for about 30 minutes.

Using a hand blender, mix for just a few seconds until thickened but still chunky. Add the fish back into the chowder and stir to reheat the fish. Ladle into deep bowls and serve hot.

Oven-Roasted Veg and Eggs

Serves four.

This is a wonderful recipe for weekend mornings. Just pop it into the oven while you have your tea or coffee. The rich, roasted flavours of the vegetables are perfectly complemented by the eggs.

- ½ red bell pepper, sliced
- ½ green bell pepper, sliced
- 1 medium aubergine, cut into bite-sized pieces
- 1 medium onion, sliced
- 1 clove garlic, chopped
- 1 medium fennel bulb, sliced
- 2 tablespoons fresh rosemary
- 2 tablespoons fresh parsley
- 3 tablespoons olive oil
- 4 large eggs

Preheat the oven to 200 C / Gas Mark 6.

Lay all of the vegetables across a roasting tin and evenly sprinkle with the rosemary and parsley. Drizzle the veg with the olive oil and toss with your hands until well coated.

Roast the vegetables in the oven for about 20 minutes or until the aubergine is tender.

Remove the vegetables from the oven and make four small depressions in them. Crack one egg into each depression and return to the oven.

Cook for another 5–10 minutes, depending on how well you like your eggs. Remove from the oven, cut into 4 portions and serve immediately.

Spicy Chicken Masala Curry

Serves four.

Why go out for an Indian lunch when you can put together this incredibly tasty curry with no trouble at all? Prepare in the evening or on a weekend and reheat for lunch throughout the week. This will keep well in the fridge for a week or you can freeze in individual containers.

- 4 tablespoons olive oil, divided
- 5 dried red chilli peppers, chopped
- 1 teaspoon coriander seeds
- 1 dessert spoon chilli powder
- 1 teaspoon poppy seeds
- 1 teaspoon cumin seeds
- 2 cloves garlic, minced
- 1 teaspoon ground cardamom
- 1 teaspoon anise seeds
- 2–3 green chilli peppers, seeded and chopped
- 1½ tablespoons tamarind paste
- 1 slice root ginger
- Small handful chopped fresh coriander
- 2 onions, chopped
- 1.5kg boneless skinless chicken thighs, diced

In a small frying pan, heat 2 tablespoons of the olive oil over a medium-high heat. Add the red chillis, coriander, chilli powder, garlic, poppy seeds, cumin, cardamom, anise and garlic. Sauté for 4–5 minutes until quite aromatic.

Let the hot chilli mixture cool to room temperature, then combine in a small bowl with the green chilli peppers, ginger, tamarind and coriander. Grind together with a pestle or heavy spoon to make a paste. Set aside.

Heat the remaining oil in a large frying pan over a medium heat and sauté the onions until browned. Add the masala mixture and sauté for another 8–10 minutes.

Add the chicken pieces, reduce the heat to low, cover and simmer for 25–30 minutes or until the chicken is cooked through.

Remove lid and bring to a boil, cook for 1 minute, then remove from the heat. Spoon into deep bowls or over roasted vegetables and serve hot.

Venison and Mushroom Pie

Serves four.

This wonderfully hearty pie uses mashed sweet potato for the crust and reheats beautifully. Bake two at a time and serve one for dinner and pack the rest into the fridge for a workday lunch.

- 2 tablespoons olive oil
- 200g small button onions, peeled
- 500g boneless haunch or shoulder of venison, diced
- 150g baby button mushrooms
- 3 celery stalks, thickly sliced
- 1 tablespoon fresh thyme
- 1 tablespoon fresh rosemary
- 300ml burgundy
- 150ml good beef stock
- 1½ teaspoons arrowroot powder
- ½ teaspoon salt
- ½ teaspoon freshly ground black pepper
- 1kg sweet potatoes, peeled and cubed
- 1 tablespoon wholegrain mustard
- Grated zest and juice of 1 orange

Heat the oil in a large saucepan over a medium heat and add the onions. Cover and cook for 4–5 minutes, stirring occasionally, until the onions are just lightly browned. Remove the onions to a plate with a slotted spoon and set aside.

Add the venison to the pan and sauté, uncovered, over a medium-high heat for 2–3 minutes or until well browned.

Add the onions, mushrooms, sliced celery, rosemary and thyme. Pour the wine and stock over all, scraping up any brown bits from the bottom of the pan. Bring to the boil and then reduce the heat to low. Cover and simmer for 45 minutes or until the meat is quite tender.

Meanwhile, boil the sweet potatoes for 15 minutes until tender. Drain, add the mustard, orange zest, orange juice, salt and pepper and mash with a fork or on low speed with a hand mixer.

Preheat the oven to 190 C / Gas Mark 5.

Blend the arrowroot powder with 2 tablespoons of cold water and whisk into the venison mixture and cook, stirring constantly, until slightly thickened.

Spoon the mixture into a 1.2 litre pie dish. Smooth the sweet potato mash over the venison mixture to cover completely. Bake for 20 minutes. To serve, scoop a healthy portion onto each plate and serve hot.

Curried Tuna and Pineapple Salad

Serves four.

This wonderful filling for avocadoes or lettuce wraps tastes even better the day after you make it. Allow it to sit overnight in the fridge before preparing your lunch.

- 1 (400g) tin tuna, drained and flaked
- 2 tablespoons olive oil mayonnaise
- 1 tablespoon curry powder
- 1 teaspoon raw honey
- ½ teaspoon salt
- ¼ teaspoon freshly ground black pepper
- 1 (220g) tin pineapple chunks, drained
- 60g cashews, roughly chopped

In a medium mixing bowl, combine the tuna, mayonnaise, curry powder, honey, salt and pepper and stir until well combined.

Stir in the pineapple chunks and cashews, cover and refrigerate overnight.

To serve, spoon ¼ of the filling into Romaine leaves or into half of a small avocado.

Tropical Coronation Chicken

Serves four.

In this variation of a classic salad dish, mangoes and cashews lend a tropical flavour to your lunch hour. You can also substitute leftover duck if you like.

- 4 skinless, boneless cooked chicken breast fillets
- 75g sultanas
- 50g toasted cashews
- ½ large mango, peeled and thinly sliced
- 6 tablespoons olive oil mayonnaise
- 1 teaspoon mild curry powder
- 1 tablespoon mango chutney
- 1 teaspoon fresh lemon juice
- ½ teaspoon salt
- ¼ teaspoon freshly ground black pepper

Cut the chicken breasts into bite-sized pieces and place in a large bowl, with the sultanas, cashews and the mango.

In a separate bowl, whisk together the mayonnaise, curry powder, chutney and lemon juice. Season with the salt and pepper, then stir gently into the chicken mixture until well blended.

Serve on a bed of salad leaves, in half an avocadoes or wrapped in a lettuce leaf.

6

PALEO DINNERS

Deliciously Simple Pot Roast

Serves six.

This is an exceptionally easy, but wonderfully flavoursome, way to prepare a nice silverside of beef. Served with a fresh green salad, dinner does not get much better than this dish.

- 1 tablespoon olive oil
- 1 (2kg) silverside roasting joint
- 1 onion, chopped
- 4 large carrots, peeled and cut into chunks
- 2 cloves garlic, minced
- 2 bay leaves
- ½ teaspoon salt, divided
- ½ teaspoon freshly ground black pepper, divided

Preheat oven to 160 C / Gas Mark 3.

Heat a casserole dish on the hob over a medium-high heat. Add the olive oil, and sear the beef joint for 4 minutes on each side until well browned. Remove the joint from the dish.

Arrange the onions, carrots, garlic, bay leaf and half of the salt and pepper in the bottom of the dish, place the meat on top and season it with the remaining salt and pepper.

Roast in the oven for 30 minutes. Reduce heat to 150 C / Gas Mark 2, and cook for an additional 1½ hours. Remove the joint to a platter and allow it to rest for 15 minutes. Slice on the diagonal before serving. To serve, place a few slices of meat on the plate, surround with the carrots and top with the onions and pan juices.

Easy Barbecued Trout

Serves two.

Nothing could be simpler or more hassle-free than this delicious recipe for fresh trout. Whether you're having a family dinner in the garden or a quick weeknight supper for two, this dish will become a favourite.

- 2 small trout, dressed and head removed
- 2 cloves garlic, chopped
- 1 lemon, sliced
- 2 sprigs fresh basil
- 2 sprigs fresh rosemary
- ½ teaspoon salt
- ¼ teaspoon freshly ground black pepper

Preheat the barbecue to a medium-high heat.

Line the cavity of each fish with half of the garlic and lemon, then tuck in the sprigs of thyme and basil. Season the tops of the fish with salt and pepper.

Wrap the fish in foil, and set on a wire rack about 15cm above the heat.

Cook for 15–20 minutes or just until fish flakes easily with a fork.

Unwrap the fish and remove the herbs and lemon. Holding the fish up by the spine, use a fork to pull the meat from the bones.

Garlic- and Lime-Glazed Chicken

Serves four.

Garlic and lime get along beautifully and turn this quick chicken dish into something special. This will taste even better the next day, so make extra to add to a luncheon salad.

- 2 tablespoons olive oil
- 4 skinless, boneless chicken breast fillets
- 4 cloves garlic, crushed
- Juice and zest of ½ large lime
- 1 teaspoon chopped fresh coriander
- ½ teaspoon salt
- ¼ teaspoon freshly ground black pepper
- 1 teaspoon raw honey
- 1 teaspoon chopped fresh parsley
- 1/2 lime, thinly sliced

Heat the oil in a large frying pan over medium heat and cut the chicken breast into bite-sized pieces.

Fry the chicken pieces in the hot oil until browned on all sides, about 7–8 minutes.

Add the garlic, lime zest and lime juice, coriander, honey, salt and pepper and continue to cook until the chicken is no longer pink in the middle, about 8–10 minutes.

Remove from the heat and spoon onto plates. Sprinkle with fresh parsley and garnish with slices of the lime.

Paleo-Friendly Courgette Frittata

Serves four.

This is a great dish to throw together on a busy weeknight. It's ready in no time and you'll never miss the cheese that's typical of a frittata.

- 225ml water
- 3 tablespoons olive oil, divided
- ½ teaspoon salt, divided
- ½ green bell pepper, seeded and chopped
- 3 courgette, cut into thin slices
- 2 cloves garlic
- 1 small red onion, diced
- 6 button mushrooms, chopped
- ½ teaspoon paprika
- 6 large eggs
- ¼ teaspoon freshly ground black pepper

Preheat oven to 180 C / Gas Mark 4.

In a large oven-safe pan over a medium-high heat, combine the water, 1 tablespoon of olive oil, ¼ teaspoon of salt, green pepper, courgette and garlic. Simmer until the courgette is tender, 5–7 minutes.

Drain off the water and discard the garlic. Stir in the onion, mushrooms, paprika, remaining salt and pepper and cook until onion is transparent. Add the eggs and stir; season with salt and pepper. Cover and cook over a low heat, without stirring, until the eggs are firm.

Salmon Fillets with Garlic and Dill

Serves six.

If you've yet to make salmon a staple in your diet, this twist on a classic recipe is a great one to convert you. Salmon is packed with protein and is a great source of omega-3 fats.

- 8 cloves garlic, peeled
- 4 tablespoons chopped fresh dill
- 100ml olive oil
- 1.3kg salmon fillets
- ½ teaspoon salt
- ½ teaspoon freshly ground black pepper

In a blender or food processor, pulse the garlic cloves and dill several times before adding the olive oil a little at a time, pulsing after each addition. You should end up with a pesto-like consistency.

Place the salmon fillets in a baking dish, skin side down. Rub the garlic mixture evenly over each piece of fish. Cover and refrigerate for at least 2 hours.

Preheat oven to 190 C / Gas Mark 5.

Season with salt and pepper. Bake the salmon fillets, uncovered, for 15–17 minutes, just until they are just cooked through. Do not over-bake or the fish will become dry.

Paleo Lancashire Hot Pot

Serves four.

Lancashire Hot Pot is one of the most satisfying things you can eat on a cool evening, but those white potatoes are off-limits. This recipes works beautifully without them, substituting cauliflower instead.

- 500g lean lamb neck fillet, trimmed and sliced
- 1 clove garlic, crushed
- 1 teaspoon beef bouillon paste
- 1 large onion, thinly sliced
- 2 leeks, thinly sliced
- 3 carrots, peeled and sliced
- 1 small head fresh cauliflower, in bite-sized pieces
- 250g fresh button or wild mushrooms, sliced
- Salt and pepper, to taste
- 1 bay leaf
- 2 sprigs of fresh thyme
- 1 sprig of fresh rosemary
- 2 tablespoons tomato purée
- 400ml lamb or chicken stock, hot

Preheat the oven to 180 C / Gas Mark 4.

In a large bowl, combine the lamb meat with the garlic and beef bouillon paste.

Arrange a layer of onions, leeks, carrots and cauliflower in the bottom of a large baking dish. Top with a layer of meat and mushrooms, then sprinkle with salt and pepper. Repeat until all ingredients have been used.

Tie the fresh herbs together with kitchen twine and place in the centre of the dish.

Mix the tomato purée into the hot stock and pour over the entire dish. Cover tightly with aluminum foil and bake for 90 minutes or until the meat is tender.

Remove the foil, turn the oven to 230 C / Gas Mark 8 and bake for another 20–25 minutes or until thickened. To serve, place a generous portion onto each plate and serve piping hot with a green salad.

Herb-Grilled Lamb Chops

Serves eight.

These lamb chops are tender, quick to cook and loaded with flavour. This recipe can also be adapted to your oven's grill if you're cooking indoors.

- 4 cloves garlic, crushed
- 4 tablespoons fresh rosemary, chopped
- 2 tablespoons fresh tarragon, chopped
- 2 tablespoons fresh thyme, chopped
- 4 tablespoons olive oil
- ½ teaspoon salt
- ¼ teaspoon freshly ground black pepper
- 8 (115g each) lamb loin chops

In a blender, combine the garlic, rosemary, tarragon and thyme and blend on a low speed as you slowly pour in the olive oil. Blend until smooth.

Season each lamb chop with salt and pepper on both sides and place in a shallow covered dish. Coat each chop with the herb paste on both sides and refrigerate, covered, for 4 hours or overnight.

Heat barbecue to high heat and place the lamb chops in a tightly wrapped foil packet.

Place on the grill and cook for 5 minutes, then turn the packet quickly over and grill for another 5 minutes. Carefully cut the foil packet open, using a knife or scissors to allow steam to escape.

Allow the lamb chops to rest for at least 5 minutes before serving.

Pork Chops Glazed with Apple Sauce

Serves four.

The classic pairing of apples and pork make this a hearty, comforting meal. Served with some sautéed spinach or a fresh salad, it's a meal you'll include on your menu regularly.

- 1 teaspoon olive oil
- 4 (170g) boneless pork loin chops
- 1 (200g) jar unsweetened apple sauce
- 250ml beef stock
- 1 teaspoon cinnamon
- 1 teaspoon salt
- ½ teaspoon chilli powder (or to taste)
- ½ teaspoon nutmeg
- 1 teaspoon minced garlic
- 1 large bay leaf

Preheat oven to 190 C / Gas Mark 5.

In a large heavy pan, heat the oil over medium heat. Add the pork chops and brown well on both sides, for about 5 minutes per side.

Mix together the apple sauce, beef stock, spices, garlic and bay leaf in a large bowl and pour over the pork chops. Bring to a simmer, then cover, reduce the heat to low and cook for an additional 30 minutes.

To serve, place a pork chop on each plate and spoon some of the apple mixture over the top of each.

Beef and Mushroom Rolls

Serves four.

Even inexpensive steak can be delicious and tender when prepared properly. This dish has plenty of flavour but costs very little to make.

For the mushroom filling:
- 15g dried porcini or chanterelle mushrooms
- 2 tablespoons olive oil
- 1 small onion, finely chopped
- 1 clove garlic, finely chopped
- 200g chestnut mushrooms, finely chopped
- 4 tablespoons finely chopped fresh parsley
- 1 teaspoon dried thyme
- ½ teaspoon salt
- ¼ teaspoon freshly ground black pepper
- Grated zest of 1 lemon

For the steak:
- 500g beef topside, cut into 8 very thin slices
- 2 tablespoon olive oil, divided
- 1 tablespoon coarsely crushed black peppercorns
- 1 onion, thinly sliced
- 2 celery sticks, sliced
- 400g sweet potatoes, scrubbed and cut into 5mm-thick slices
- 2 carrots, peeled and sliced
- 300ml beef stock
- 4 tablespoons dry sherry
- 1 bay leaf

Make the mushroom filling:

Place the dried mushrooms in a heat-proof dish, cover with boiling water and allow them to soak for 15 minutes or until soft. Drain the mushrooms and chop finely. Set aside.

Heat the 2 tablespoons of olive oil for the stuffing in a large heavy pan over medium heat. Add the onion and garlic and cook, stirring frequently, for 5–6 minutes, until just golden brown.

Add the chestnut mushrooms and sauté for 3 minutes, stirring occasionally, then stir in the mushrooms and the remaining stuffing ingredients. Remove from heat and allow to cool for five minutes.

Make the steak:
Lay the beef slices between sheets of waxed paper and pound out as thinly as possible with a rolling pin.

Divide the stuffing equally among the beef slices, then roll up each slice and secure in place with a toothpick.

Lightly brush the beef rolls with a little olive oil, then roll them in the crushed peppercorns on a plate.

In a large heavy frying pan, heat the remaining olive oil over a medium heat and brown the beef rolls on all sides, about 3 minutes per side. Remove from the pan and set aside.

Add the onion and celery to the skillet, reduce and sauté for about 5 minutes until tender. Add the sweet potatoes and carrots and cook, stirring frequently, for 5 minutes before returning the beef rolls to the skillet.

Pour in the beef stock and sherry and add the bay leaf. Bring to the boil, then reduce heat to low, cover and simmer for 20 minutes until the meat and vegetables are both tender.

Remove the beef rolls from the pan and increase the heat to high. Boil the liquid and vegetables until slightly thickened, about 5 minutes. To serve, place a roll onto each plate, top with vegetables and sauce and garnish with fresh parsley, if desired.

7

PALEO DESSERTS

Ginger-Glazed Pears with Walnuts

Makes six.

Dessert is sometimes best served as something light and fruity, even on cooler evenings. This recipe is very simple to make, and if you prepare it in autumn, the pears will be at the peak of their flavour.

- 3 large, firm but ripe dessert pears
- 30g preserved stem ginger in syrup, drained and finely chopped
- 2 teaspoons raw honey
- 1 teaspoon lemon juice
- 3 tablespoons ginger syrup (from the jar of stem ginger)
- 50g sultanas
- 50g chopped walnuts
- 4 sprigs fresh mint for garnish

Preheat the grill to moderate.

Cut the pears into quarters lengthways. Peel and then gently scoop out the core with a spoon. Arrange the pear quarters on their backs on the rack of a grill pan.

Whisk together the stem ginger, honey, lemon juice and ginger syrup, and brush onto the pears.

In a small bowl, combine the sultanas and walnuts and gently press into each indentation left by the cores, mounding the mixture up a bit in each one until all is used.

Grill for 5–7 minutes or until just slightly browned.

To serve, arrange the pears on serving plates. Drizzle any remaining syrup over the pears and garnish with the sprigs of fresh mint.

Berrylicious Ice Lollies

Makes twelve.

This is a great snack or dessert to make ahead and keep in the freezer for those days when you crave a sweet. They come together in a jiffy without any cooking and are wonderful made with any seasonal berries.

- 350g blueberries
- 375g strawberries, hulled
- 2 teaspoons raw honey
- 600ml vanilla soya milk
- Pinch of nutmeg

Arrange 12 small paper cups on a baking sheet.

Combine all of the ingredients in a blender or food processor and blend on high until smooth.

Divide the mixture between the paper cups, filling 2/3 full.

Place on a flat surface in the freezer for 2 hours. Gently insert an ice lolly stick into the centre of each one, stopping just shy of the bottom.

Continue freezing for another 2 hours or until firmly set.

To eat, hold the stick in one hand and gently twist off the cup with the other. If the cup won't come away easily, pass it under warm running water once or twice and try again.

Strawberry and Kiwi Granita with Strawberry Sauce

Serves six.

A granita is similar to a sorbet, but with a more icy texture. It's a delicious way to use fruits in season and can be made with almost any ripe fruit.

- 500g ripe strawberries, sliced
- 2 medium kiwi, peeled and chopped
- 3 teaspoons raw honey
- 240ml unsweetened apple juice
- Additional strawberries or fresh mint leaves to garnish

Put the strawberries and kiwi in a bowl, pour the honey over all and allow to sit at room temperature for 30 minutes.

Place the fruit mixture into a food processor or blender and blend on high until smooth. Measure out 150ml of the purée and set aside to be used as the sauce.

Mix the remaining purée with the apple juice and pour into a shallow metal tray or baking pan. Freeze for about 30 minutes or until the mixture has begun to set round the edges.

Use a fork to scrape the partially set mixture from the edges into the liquid centre. Return to the freezer and freeze for a further 20 minutes. Scrape the set edges into the centre again, and then return to the freezer. Repeat this 2–3 times until the consistency is that of fluffy crystals.

To serve, divide the granita into 6 dessert dishes, pour some of the sauce over and garnish with reserved berries or sprigs of fresh mint.

Easy Mango Sorbet

Serves four.

Mango is a treasure amongst the tropical fruits. It's loaded with antioxidants and fibre and is readily available in most markets. Be sure to use nicely ripened mangoes rather than overripe ones, as the latter become too soft and watery.

- 2 mangoes, peeled, stones removed and cubed
- 2 tablespoons raw honey
- 250ml cream of coconut
- 1 cup of ice

Place the cubed mangoes, honey, cream of coconut and ice into a blender; puree until smooth.

Pour the mixture into a large plastic freezer bag. Seal and freeze on a flat surface for 45 minutes to 1 hour. Every 15 minutes or so during freezing, massage the bag to redistribute the contents.

To serve, scoop into dessert dishes and eat at once.

Paleo Pumpkin Pie

Serves six to eight.

This creamy and deliciously spicy pumpkin pie is completely Paleo friendly, using almond milk and hazelnut flour to create a dessert that is every bit as good as the traditional version, if not better.

For the pastry:
- 180g hazelnut flour
- 1 teaspoon salt
- 120ml coconut oil, melted
- 2 tablespoons almond milk

For the pie filling:
- 500g pumpkin puree
- 250ml almond milk
- 100ml maple syrup
- 4 tablespoons arrowroot powder
- 1 tablespoon raw honey
- 1 teaspoon ground cinnamon
- ½ teaspoon ground ginger
- ½ teaspoon ground nutmeg
- ½ teaspoon salt
- ¼ teaspoon ground cloves

Make the pastry:

Preheat oven to 220 C / Gas Mark 7.

Stir together the hazelnut flour and salt.

In a separate mixing bowl, whisk together the coconut oil and almond milk until creamy. Pour oil mixture into flour mixture and stir with fork just until well blended.

Press the pastry into the bottom and sides of a 23cm quiche dish. Bake for 15 minutes in a preheated oven. Remove and set aside.

Make the pie filling:

Decrease the oven temperature to 180 C / Gas Mark 4.

Place pumpkin puree, almond milk, maple syrup, arrowroot, honey, cinnamon, ginger, nutmeg, salt and cloves in a blender and blend on medium speed until well combined.

Pour into the pastry and wrap edges with aluminum foil to prevent them from getting too brown.

Bake for 60 minutes or until a toothpick inserted in the centre comes out clean.

Cool the pie to room temperature for 2 hours, then refrigerate overnight before serving.

Paleo Pear Cakes

Makes eight cakes.

These little cakes are rich and moist, with a delicate pear flavour. Use very ripe pears for these to get the best flavour and the desired moistness.

- 100g hazelnut flour
- 1 teaspoon gluten-free baking powder
- ½ teaspoon bicarbonate of soda
- 1 pear, peeled and grated
- 4 tablespoons coconut oil, melted
- 115ml raw honey

Preheat oven to 190 C / Gas Mark 5.

In a medium mixing bowl, mix together the flour, bicarbonate of soda and baking powder.

Add the grated pear. Mix well. Add the oil and honey and beat on low speed with a hand mixer or for about 1 minute by hand.

Divide into paper cases and bake for 25 minutes. Allow to cool to room temperature before serving or placing into plastic resealable bags.

Creamy Vanilla Shake

Serves two.

If you're feeling a craving for a smooth milkshake, this creamy vanilla shake can come to your rescue. It takes just a few moments to prepare and will satisfy your cravings without hurting your health.

- 500ml coconut milk
- 1 teaspoon pure vanilla extract
- 2 teaspoons raw honey or 1 teaspoon maple syrup
- ¼ teaspoon nutmeg
- 8–10 ice cubes

In a blender, combine the coconut milk, vanilla extract, honey and nutmeg. Blend on high until smooth and well blended.

Add the ice cubes and blend on high until very smooth and thick.

Pour into glasses and garnish with additional nutmeg, if desired.

Berry Tart

Serves six to eight.

This tart takes just a few minutes to prepare, but it tastes wonderful enough for to use for a dinner party. This is an especially good dessert for summer, when berries are at their peak.

For the filling:	For the crust:
• 1kg blueberries	• 350g almond flour
• 1kg strawberries, sliced	• ¼ teaspoon baking soda
• 500ml unsweetened apple juice	• ½ teaspoon cinnamon
• Juice of 1 lemon	• ½ teaspoon nutmeg
• 1 teaspoon arrowroot powder	• 120ml coconut oil, melted
	• 1 teaspoon pure vanilla extract

Make the filling:
Preheat oven to 180 C / Gas Mark 4.

In a heavy saucepan over medium heat, simmer the berries, apple juice, lemon juice and arrowroot powder for 15 minutes, stirring and mashing berries frequently.

Make the crust:
While the berries are simmering, combine all ingredients for the crust together in a large bowl.

Press into a pie plate and bake for 10 minutes. Remove from the oven and allow to cool for 5 minutes.

Scoop the berry mixture into the crust and refrigerate for 1 hour before serving.

Orange Dream Smoothie

Serves four.

Enjoy this take on a classic American treat, which is also very good for you. It will separate quickly, so drink it immediately.

- 1 litre fresh orange juice
- 1 litre almond milk
- 1 teaspoon vanilla extract
- 3 tablespoons honey
- 6 ice cubes

Combine all the ingredients except the ice in a blender and blend until smooth.

Add the ice cubes and blend until thick and creamy.

To serve, pour into tall glasses.

Mixed-Fruit Compote

Serves six.

This compote combines a variety of dried fruits to create a treat that is as nutritious as it is comforting. This keeps well for up to a week and reheats very well.

- 470ml fresh-squeezed orange juice
- 240ml unsweetened pineapple juice
- 1 teaspoon cinnamon
- 1 teaspoon ginger
- ½ teaspoon ground cloves
- 225g dried cherries
- 225g sultanas
- 225g prunes
- 225g figs
- 225g dried apricots
- 225g slivered almonds

In a large saucepan, combine the orange juice, pineapple juice, cinnamon, ginger and cloves and simmer over medium-high heat just until it reaches the boil.

Add all of the fruits and simmer for about 10 minutes. Serve warm and sprinkled with almonds.

8

PALEO SNACKS

Nutty Stuffed Dates

Makes twelve pieces.

Dates give you a tremendous solution to a sweet tooth without you trashing your healthy diet. This recipe calls for stuffing the dates with nuts, adding crunch and healthy fats to your snack.

- 12 pitted dates
- 30g chopped black walnuts
- 3 tablespoons red wine
- 4 tablespoons raw honey
- Freshly ground black pepper, to taste

Place the dates onto a cutting board or clean surface and stuff the empty pits with the walnuts. Arrange in a single layer in a non-stick frying pan.

In a small bowl, combine the wine and honey and microwave for 10–15 seconds just until warm. Whisk until well blended and then pour over the dates.

Sprinkle with the pepper and cook over medium heat until the skins begin to peel away from the dates. Place the dates on a serving dish, and allow to cool slightly before serving.

Summer Berry Salad

Serves six.

Berries are a great pick-me-up snack, especially in the summer months. This salad keeps well for several days, so make up a batch and take it to work or the gym in plastic containers.

- 375g strawberries, quartered
- 350g blueberries
- 275g blackberries
- 300g raspberries
- 100g red currants
- 3 tablespoons finely chopped fennel greens
- 1 teaspoon crushed fresh mint
- 2 tablespoons raw honey

Combine all of the berries in a large mixing bowl, tossing gently with your hands to blend.

In a small bowl, combine the fennel and mint with a fork.

In another small dish, heat the raw honey in the microwave for 10–15 seconds, just until warm and thinned out. Allow to cool to just slightly warm before stirring into the herbs.

Toss the honey and herb mixture with the berries until well incorporated. Cover and refrigerate for at least 4 hours before serving. Serve cold or at room temperature.

Curried Fruit and Nut Mix

Serves six.

This snack mix is delightfully different from traditional fruit and nut blends. The curry lends just a hint of heat and spice that is beautifully paired with the sweet tang of the fruit. This is a great snack for packed lunches, both at school and at work.

- 225g walnut pieces
- 225g cashew halves
- 225g sultanas
- 225g dried apricots, roughly chopped
- 225g dried apples, roughly chopped
- 2 tablespoons melted coconut oil
- 2 teaspoons mild curry powder
- 1 teaspoon paprika

Preheat oven to 180 C / Gas Mark 4 and line a baking sheet with aluminum foil.

In a large mixing bowl, combine the walnuts, cashews, sultanas, apricots and apples and toss with both hands to blend.

In a small measuring jug, whisk together the coconut oil, curry powder and paprika and pour over the fruit and nut mixture.

Blend well with your hands or a large spoon until the fruit and nuts are fairly evenly coated.

Spread out into a thin layer on the baking sheet (use 2 if necessary) and bake for 20–25 minutes or just until the mixture is slightly browned. Cool completely before sealing in plastic bags or an airtight jar.

Sweet Glazed Walnuts

Serves eight.

This is a great treat to pack into lunches or take with you to the gym or park. These will keep well in an airtight container for up to two weeks, but you may well finish them before then.

- 500g walnut halves
- 100ml raw honey
- 2 teaspoons ground cinnamon
- 6 tablespoons almond milk
- ¼ teaspoon salt
- 1 teaspoon vanilla extract

Preheat oven to 180 C / Gas Mark 4.

Spread nuts in a single layer on a large baking sheet. Roast for 8–10 minutes or just until the nuts start to turn brown. Remove from the oven.

Stir together the honey, cinnamon, salt and almond milk in a medium saucepan.

Cook over a medium-high heat for 7–8 minutes or until the mixture reaches the soft ball stage. (113 C)

Remove from heat, and stir in vanilla immediately.

Add the walnuts to the syrup, and stir well until evenly coated. Spoon onto waxed paper, and immediately separate with a fork. Cool to room temperature before storing in an airtight container.

Nutty Banana Lollies

Serves four.

These ice lollies are a huge hit with the children, but adults love them just as much. They're a wonderfully nutritious snack any time of day. Use green-tipped bananas, as they will hold their shape better.

- 4 medium, just-ripe bananas
- 4 tablespoons almond butter
- 100g chopped unsalted cashews
- 4 ice lolly sticks

Peel the bananas and trim off one end to make the bottom of the banana flat. Insert an ice lolly stick halfway up the centre of each banana.

In a small bowl, combine the almond butter and cashews and then use a spatula or the back of a spoon to spread fairly evenly around all sides of each banana, placing each one on a baking sheet lined with waxed paper.

Once all of the bananas are coated, place into the freezer for at least 1 hour. Once frozen, wrap in individual sheets of waxed paper to store for up to 1 week.

Paleo-Friendly Banana Muffins

Makes ten muffins.

These rich and moist banana muffins are every bit as delicious as the traditional version. They keep well in an airtight container for up to a week, so they make great snacks for packed lunches.

- 110ml raw honey
- 110ml melted coconut oil
- 2 large eggs
- 3 large ripe bananas
- 225g almond flour
- 1 teaspoon gluten-free baking powder
- ½ teaspoon salt
- 75g sultanas

Preheat the oven to 190 C / Gas Mark 5.

Mix the coconut oil and honey together in a large bowl with a hand mixer until well blended. Add the 2 eggs and mix well on medium speed until you have a smooth airy mixture.

Mash the bananas one at a time and add them to the mixing bowl, mixing after each addition.

Mix the almond flour, baking powder and salt together in a separate bowl and then add them, a bit at a time to the wet ingredients. Gently fold in the sultanas.

Spoon into muffin cases, making each case about 2/3 full.

Bake for 20–25 minutes or until golden brown. Allow to cool for 10–15 minutes before serving and cool to room temperature before storing in an airtight container.

Easy Kale Crisps

Serves four.

Crisps made with kale are delicately crispy and so delicious. They're much better for you than even the "healthy" crisps sold in stores.

- 2 bunches (about 450g) fresh kale, rinsed and dried
- 1 teaspoon sea salt
- 1 teaspoon paprika
- ½ teaspoon freshly ground black pepper
- 2 tablespoons light olive oil

Turn oven to lowest heat setting.

Tear the kale into pieces no less than 10cm long (they shrink quite a bit during drying) and place into a large mixing bowl.

Combine the olive oil, sea salt, paprika and pepper and pour over the kale.

Using your hands, toss the kale well so that it is fairly evenly coated.

Spread the kale onto as many large baking sheets as you need to keep them in a single layer, and bake for 20 minutes. Gently turn each leaf over and bake for another 10 minutes or until crisp.

Banana Chips

Serves two.

Banana chips are a delicious snack popular in both Latin and Indian cuisines. They're much tastier made at home than the stale product sold in packets in the shops.

- 1 cup coconut oil
- 2 mostly green bananas, sliced
- ¼ teaspoon ground turmeric
- ½ teaspoon salt

Heat the coconut oil in a deep, heavy saucepan over medium-high heat. When a small piece of a banana tip sizzles in the oil, then it's ready for you to begin cooking.

Add about 1/2 of the banana slices to the pan and use tongs or a slotted spoon to separate the chips from each other as they cook. Cook for 2–3 minutes or until golden.

Remove cooked chips and dust with the turmeric and salt, tossing carefully to season each chip.

Serve hot.

Spicy Devilled Eggs

Serves four.

Devilled eggs are a tasty treat any time of day, though they're especially popular at barbecues and picnics. These are extra spicy and completely Paleo friendly.

- 6 large eggs, hard boiled and peeled
- 2 tablespoons olive oil mayonnaise
- 1 teaspoon spicy brown mustard
- 1 teaspoon chopped fresh dill
- ½ teaspoon cumin
- ¼ teaspoon salt
- ¼ teaspoon freshly ground black pepper
- ½ teaspoon paprika

Slice the boiled eggs in half lengthwise and place the whites onto a platter and the yolks into a small mixing bowl. Using a fork, mash the yolks until they are almost powdery in appearance.

To the yolks, add the olive oil mayonnaise, mustard, dill, cumin, salt and pepper. Mix well.

Spoon about 1 tablespoon of the yolk mixture into each egg white half until all is used. Sprinkle with paprika and refrigerate for at least 1 hour before serving.

Salmon and Avocado Spread

Serves four to six.

The buttery creaminess of a ripe avocado is the perfect foil for salty salmon. This recipe is wonderful to use as a dip, a spread for crackers or even as a sandwich filling.

- 170g sliced smoked salmon
- 1 small ripe avocado, peeled and pitted
- ½ teaspoon mild curry powder
- ½ teaspoon freshly ground black pepper
- 100g chopped red onion
- 1 teaspoon fresh lemon juice

Combine the salmon, avocado, curry powder and black pepper in a food processor and pulse just once or twice. Alternately, blend by hand with a fork or whisk until it is still slightly chunky but beginning to break down.

Fold in the onions and squeeze the lemon juice over all. Cover and refrigerate for 1 hour or more before serving.

Paleo Sweet Potato Crisps

Serves six.

These sweet potato chips have just enough salt to satisfy cravings, and oven frying in olive oil provides a healthier crunch.

- 4 large sweet potatoes, peeled
- 2 tablespoons olive oil
- 1 teaspoon salt
- 1/2 teaspoon freshly ground black pepper

Preheat the oven to 150 C / Gas Mark 2.

Slice the sweet potatoes on a mandolin into thin discs.

Combine the olive oil, salt and pepper. Pour over the potatoes and toss.

Spread the chips onto baking sheets in a single layer and bake for about 40–50 minutes or until very dry and crisp.